Dragon

Gordon Winch & Gregory Blaxell
Illustrated by Joe Spellman

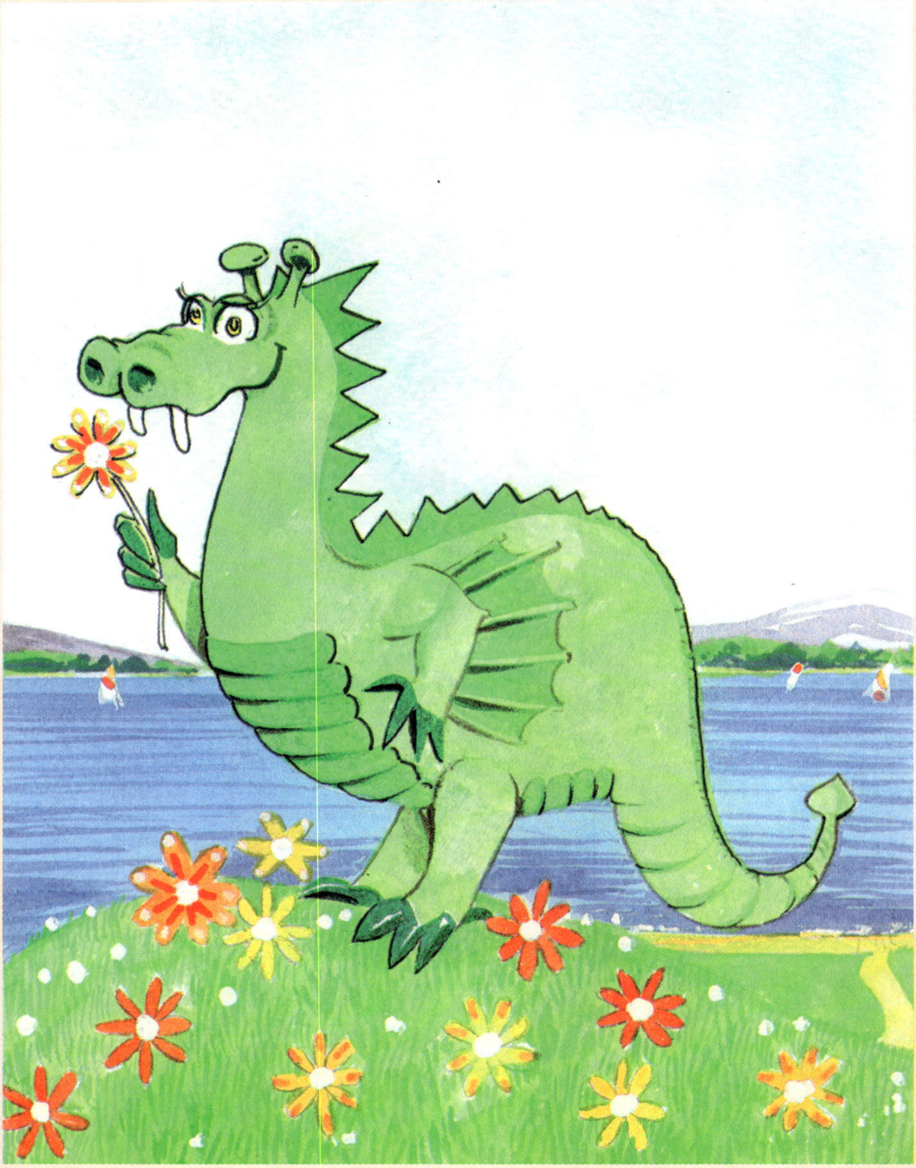

A green dragon

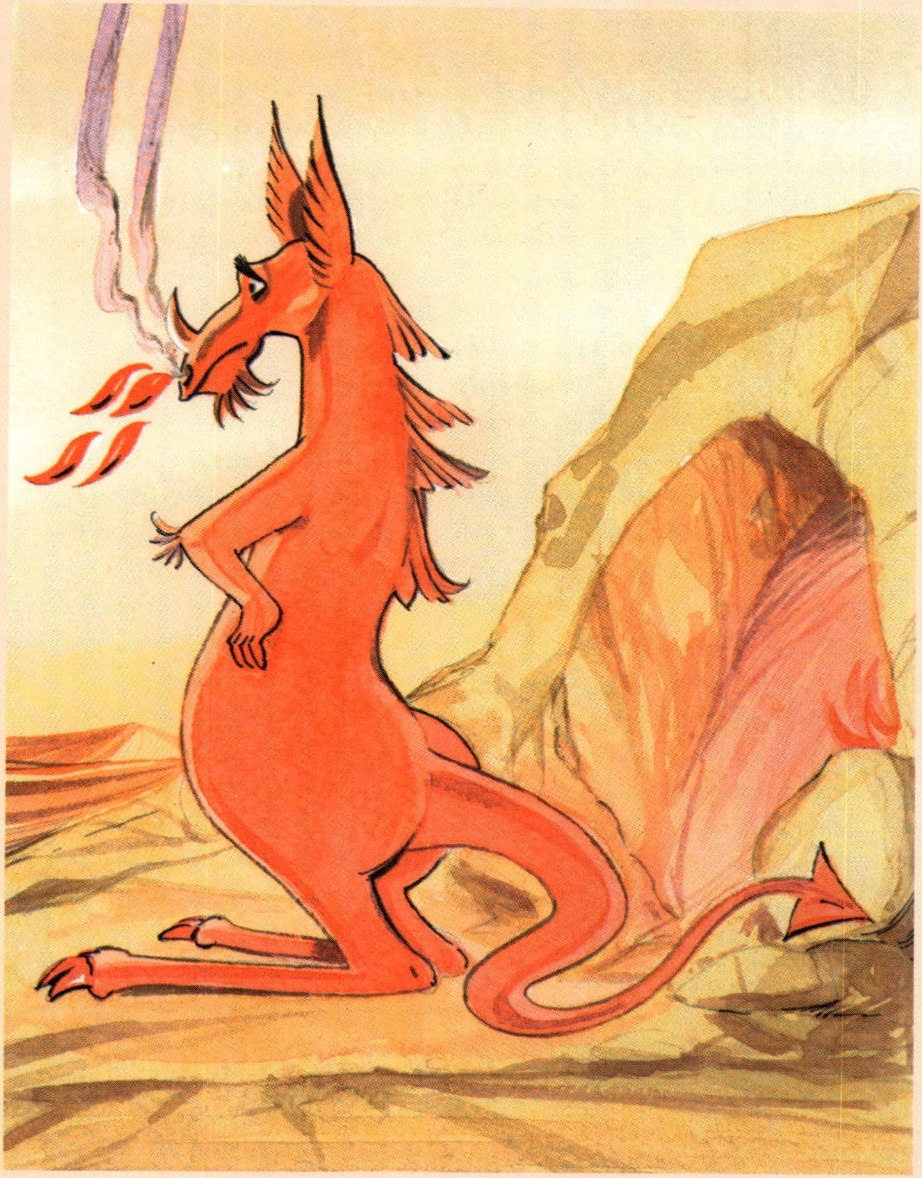

A red dragon

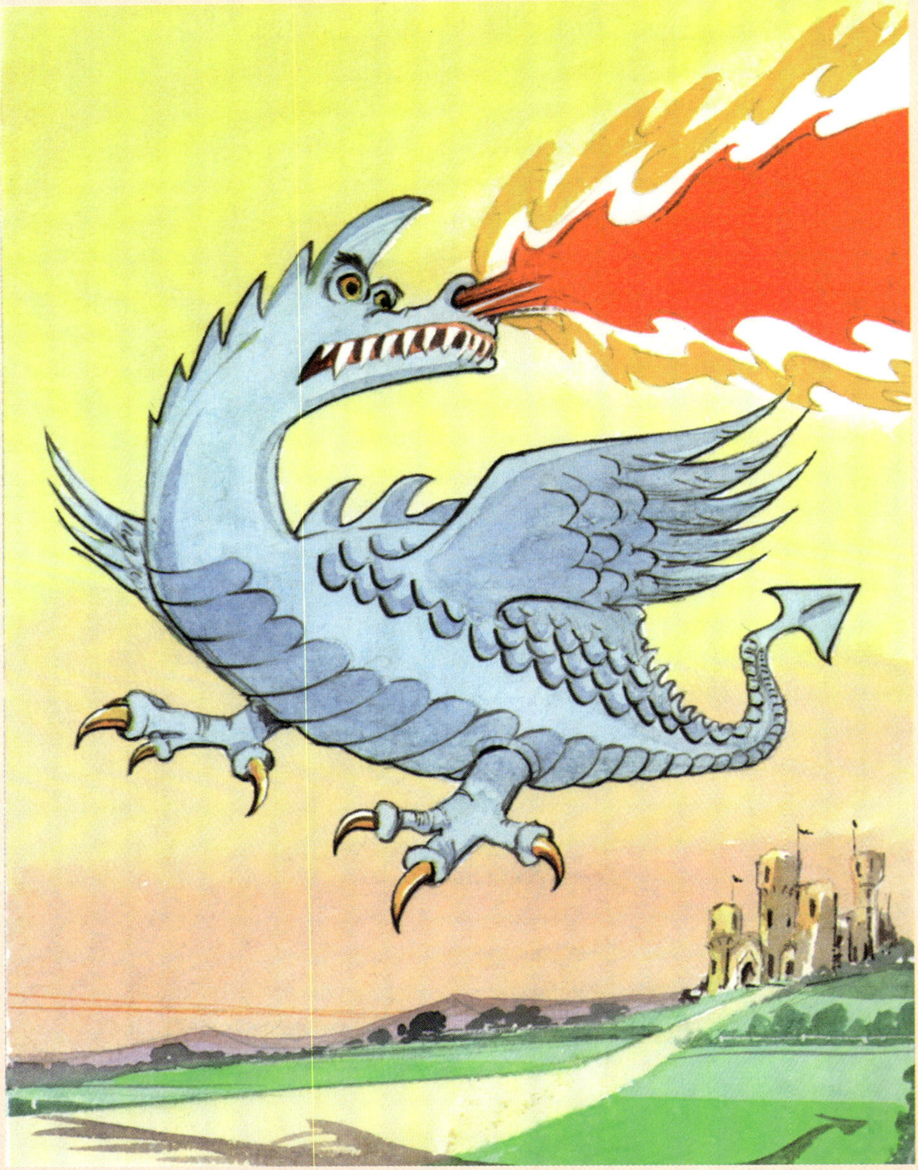

A blue dragon

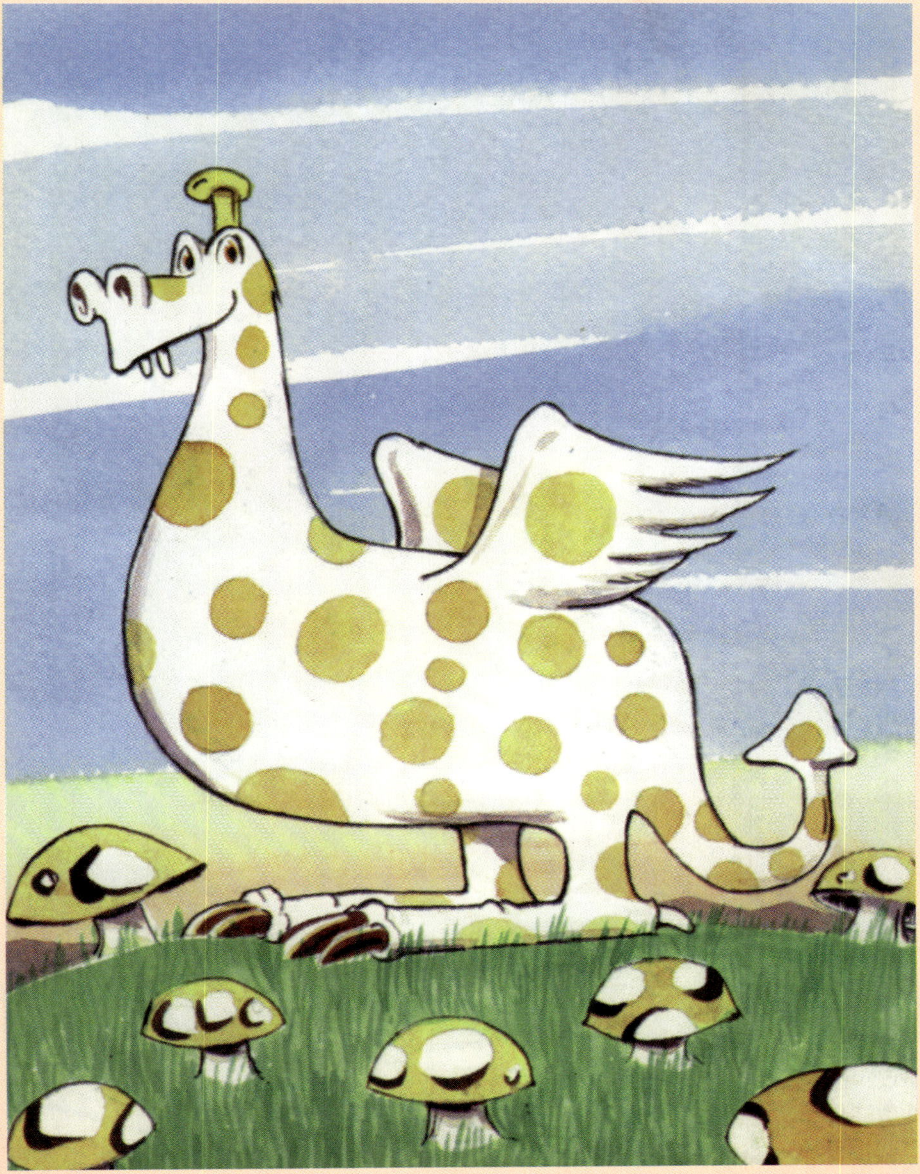

A spotted dragon

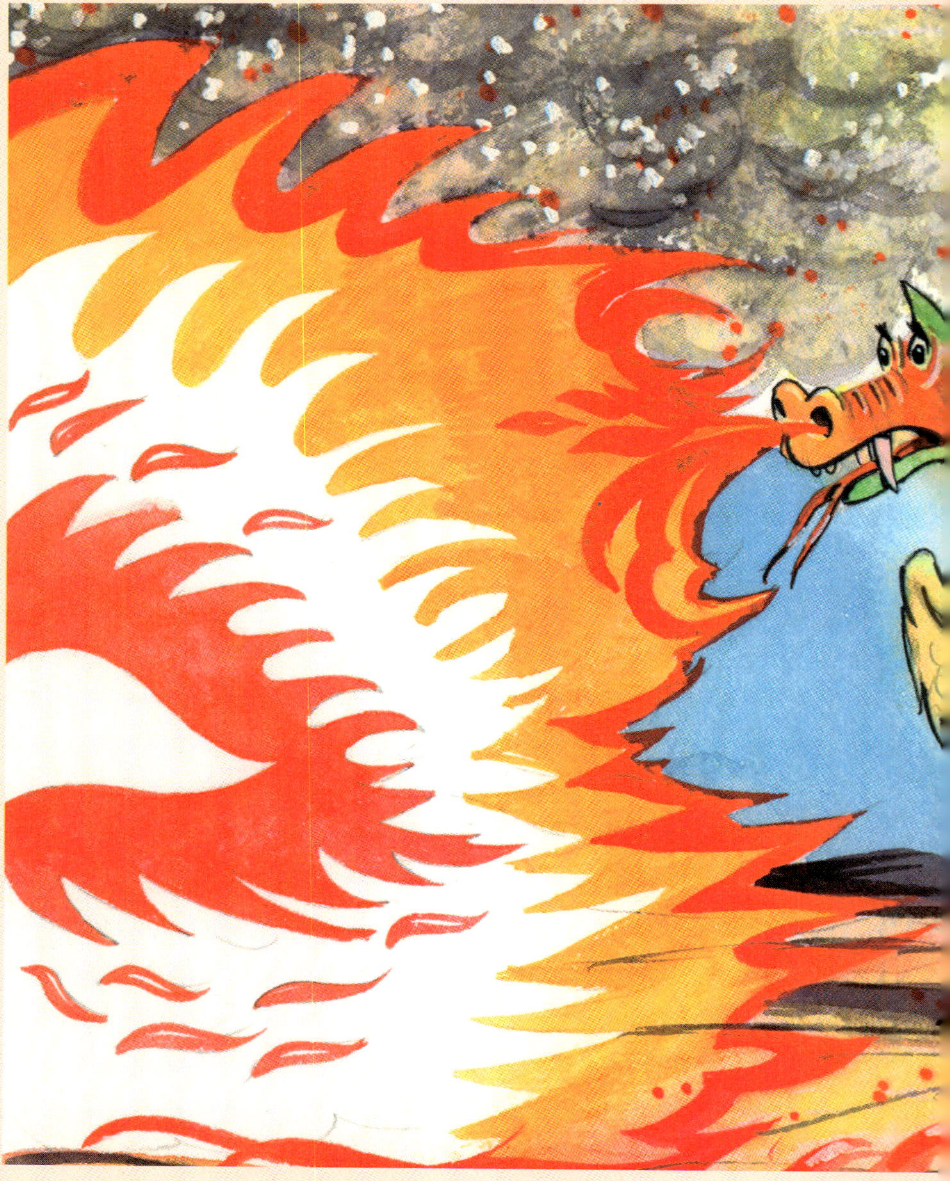

A fiery dragon

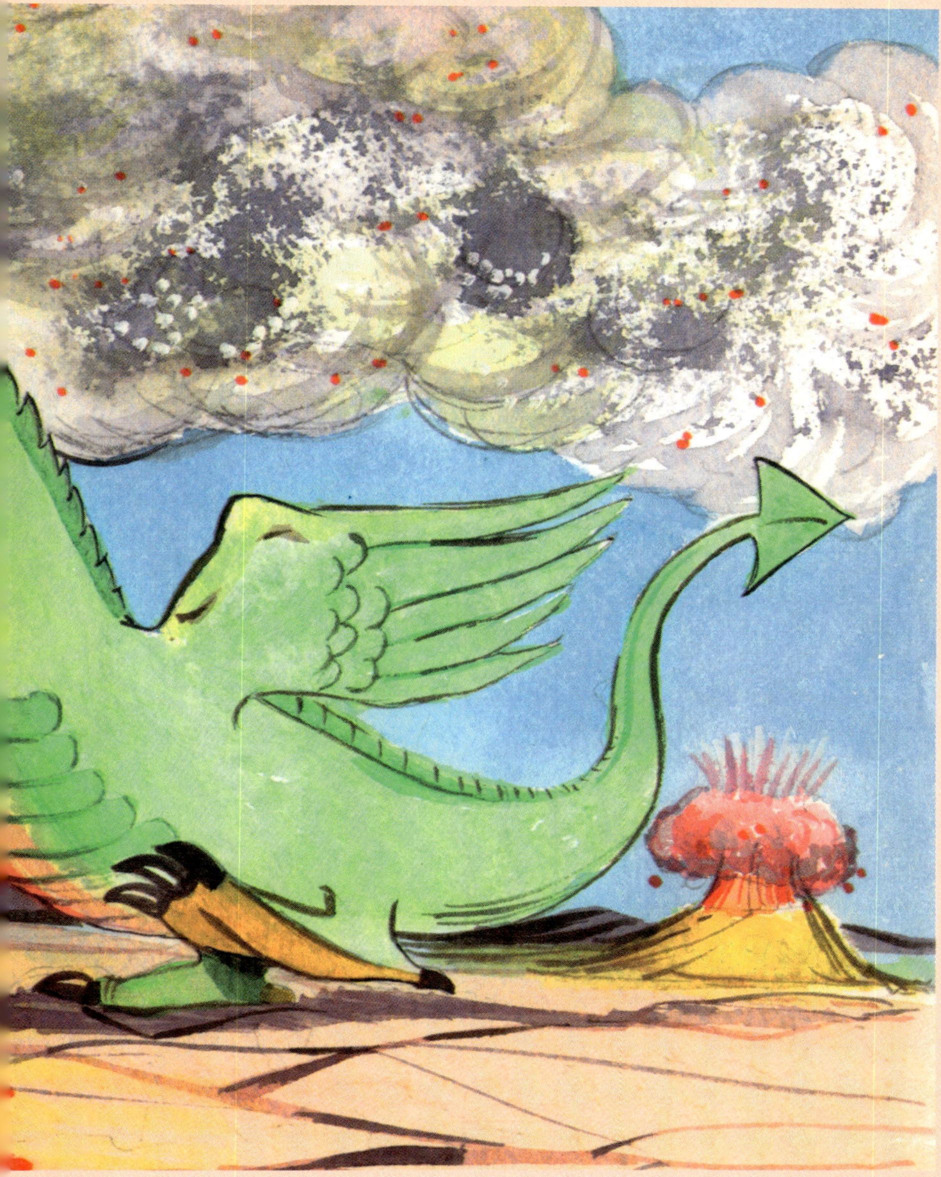

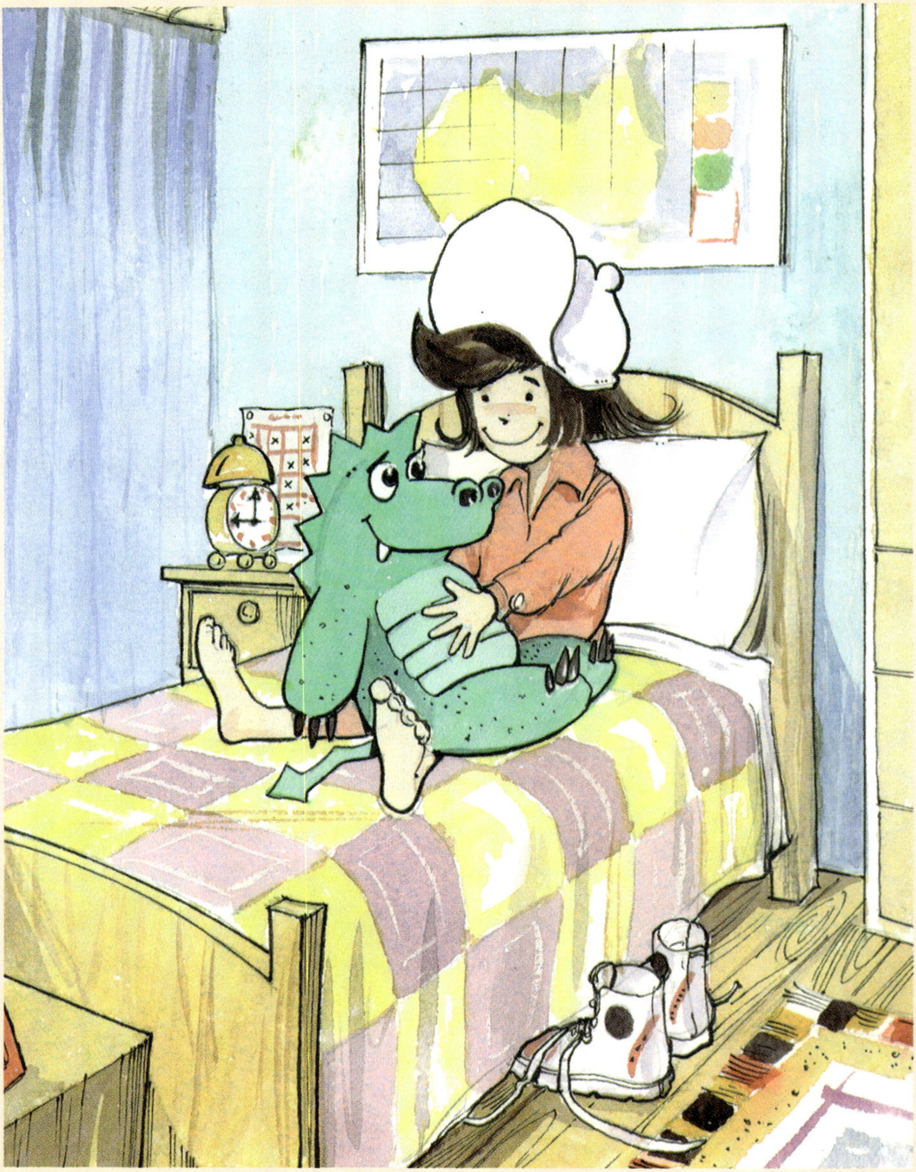

A pet dragon